This book belongs to :

HAVING BIG DREAMS!
What does it take to become...?

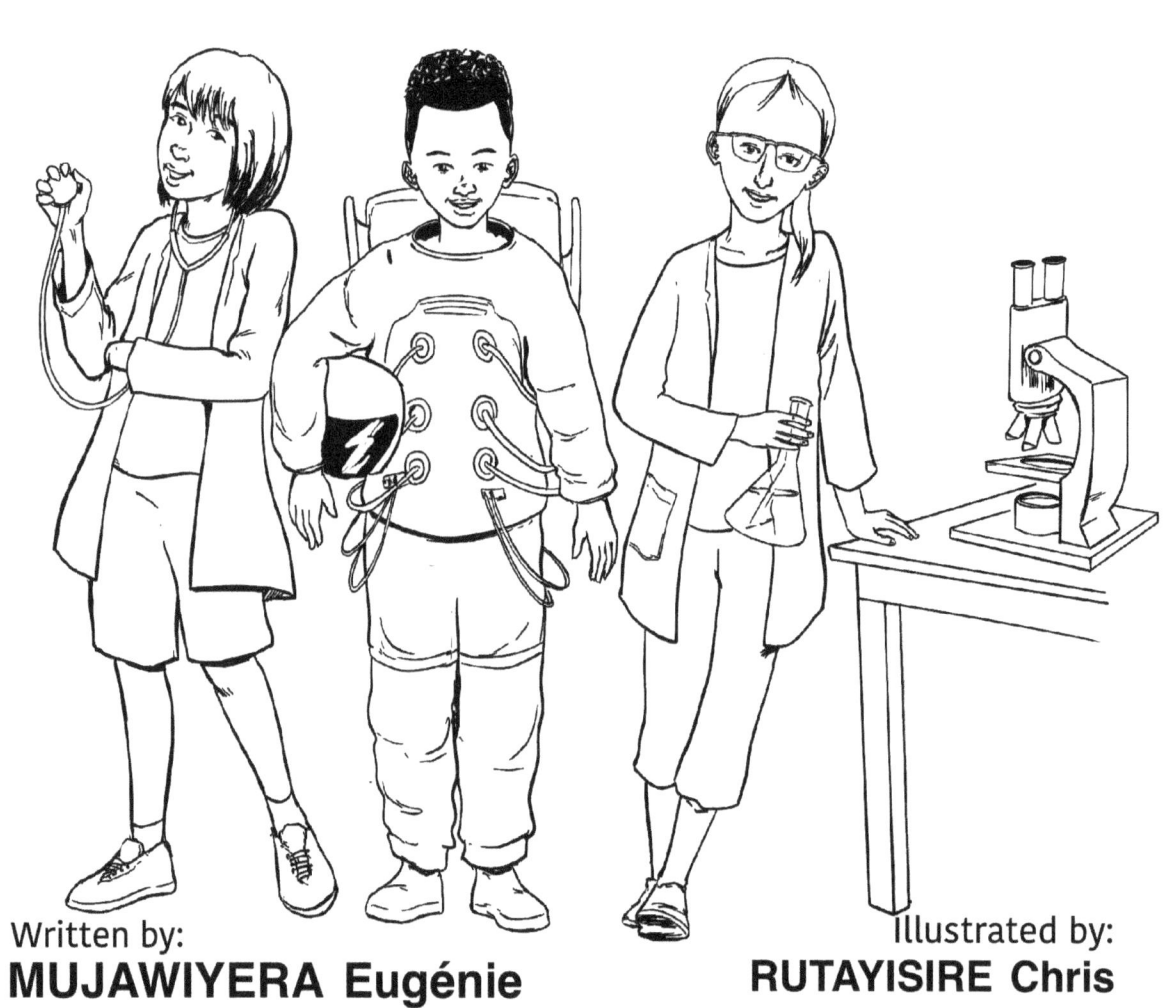

Written by:
MUJAWIYERA Eugénie

Illustrated by:
RUTAYISIRE Chris

I want to thank Roxanna K., Joy M., Elvis M., Molo M., who helped me create this amazing book.

You are awesome!

Bill and Haneul: Hi Angela!

Angela: Hi Bill and Haneul! How are you?

Bill and Haneul: We are fine, thank you.

Angela: What are you doing in this park?

Haneul: We are asking ourselves questions about what we want to be when we grow up.

Angela: Ah, that's super interesting! So, tell us Haneul, what would you like to be when you grow up?

Haneul: Hmmm... I'd like to be a medical doctor.

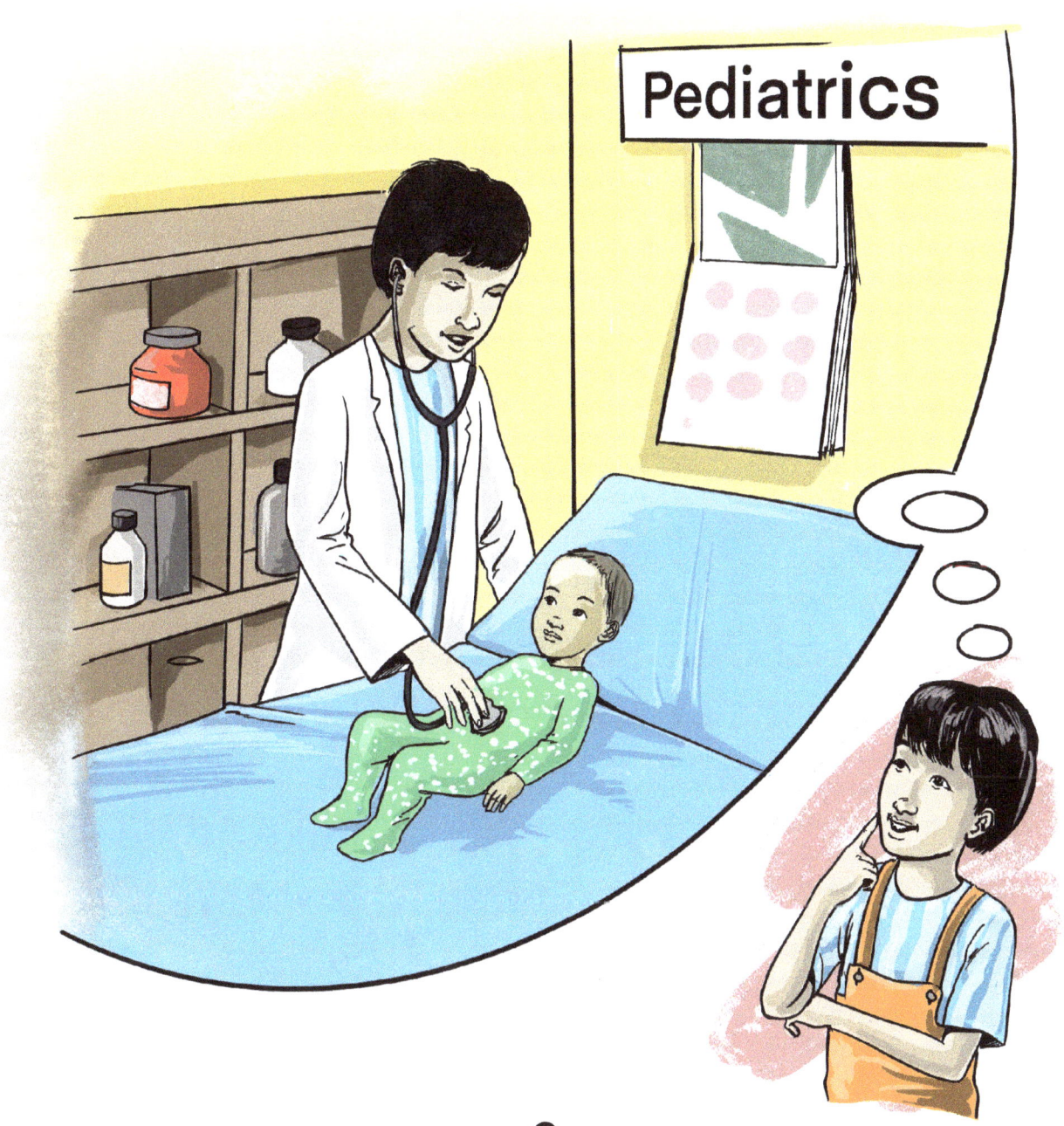

Angela: Why a medical doctor?

Haneul: Well... because I really like helping people! I think being a doctor is the best thing in the world! When someone is a medical doctor, he/she can help people who are suffering.

Bill: I learned that medical doctors have different types of specializations.

Haneul: Yes, that's true. Me, I'd like to be a pediatrician! That's a doctor who treats babies, children, youth and teenagers.

Bill: Fantastic! Great idea! Pediatrician! I hope you know that babies cry a lot.

Haneul: Yes, I am ready to follow my dream. I can put up with anything.

Angela: And you, Bill, what would you like to be when you grow up?

Bill: I would like to be a great scientist, maybe an astronomer or an astronaut.

Angela: Why? Do not tell me it's to fight with aliens!

Bill: Haha, yes, maybe that too. Maybe, I will get a chance to see the aliens! I dream that one day, I will work with the International Space Station (ISS) because astronomy fascinates me.

Haneul: Astronomy! That is so cool!

Bill: Yes, I am always fascinated by the sun, stars and planets! Astronomy is the science that studies the stars and celestial bodies.

Angela: Bill, you know that to be a great astronomer or astronaut, you have to work hard and read a lot of Science books.

Bill: I totally agree with you. Angela, you know after elementary school we will go to high school and after high school we will go to university. What would you like to do when you finish high school?

Angela: After high school, I absolutely have to go to university. I would like to be a researcher in Biology!

Bill: What do biology researchers do?

Angela: First of all, let me explain what Biology is. It is the science that studies life and living things. A Biology researcher does research related to Biology (living organisms). His or her goal is to advance Science.

Haneul: Oh cool! You know, I have a little sister who is always telling me that she would like to be a pilot later. Maybe she could take us around the world.

Bill: That's a great idea! At home, my older brother told us that he dreams of being a lawyer.

Haneul: Seriously, the world needs lawyers. Let me give you an example of when a mean person falsely accused my father's friend of stealing money from him, my uncle Dae-Jung who is a lawyer defended him!

Angela: Wow, that lawyer really saved your father's friend! To be a lawyer, he sure did study a lot at the university, but I don't know exactly how many years.

Haneul: Well, I have two cousins who are at university. One is studying to be a cardiologist and the other wants to be an architect.

Bill: Great! Maybe the cardiologist can help my grandmother if her heart hurts.

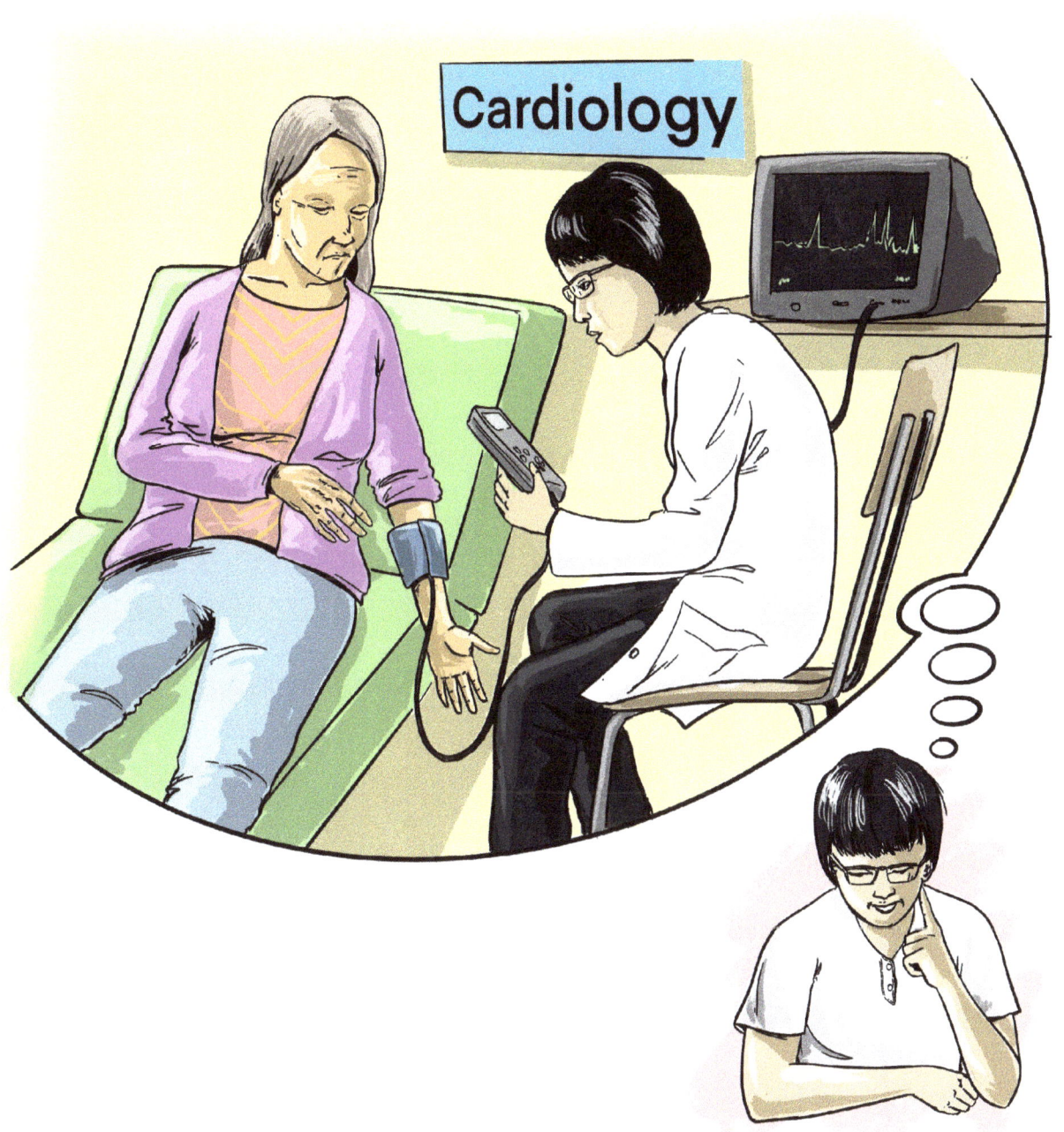

Angela: And the architect will be able to help me design a big, beautiful laboratory where I can conduct all my experiments!

Bill: Your cousins **have big dreams**! Ah, I wonder how many years it takes to become a doctor, science researcher, lawyer, pilot, architect or whatever. We can ask that question to an older student!

Haneul: Oh, I have an idea! Let's talk to Aya. She is Bill's older sister, she is in grade 11 and, she is 17. She is very smart and kind, her advice can be reliable. I always see her after school when she picks up Bill.

Haneul: Let us meet at 3:45 in the afternoon, in front of the main gate. We will ask permission from our parents so we can chat with her for a few minutes.

Bill: Okay, there is no problem, she will pick me up after school.

After a few hours, Aya meets them at the main entrance.

Aya: Are you all okay?

Angela and Haneul: Yes, we are fine, thank you!

Angela: Thank you for giving us some of your time. We have a few questions related to higher education. How many years does it take to become a doctor, astronomer, pilot, lawyer, biologist or whatever? Also, can you give us some advice of what we need to do to be successful in our studies?

Aya: Interesting questions! Let's take the example of a doctor. To be a general practitioner, you have to go through several stages. After primary and secondary school, you have to go to university, choose the faculty of medicine. It can take between 6 and 7 years, it depends on the country, but that is not all. After general medicine, doctors can go further and do specializations like pediatrics, cardiology, neurology, etc. Specialization in medicine also takes more years of study, maybe between 3 and 5 years. In total, to be a medical specialist can take between 9 and 12 years of university.

You have to work hard in elementary and high school first. I would also say that in the classroom, you have to be disciplined, have good habits and good behaviour! You have to be courageous and motivated. Being well organized is a necessary part of being successful in life. You must always do your homework, do research online or in the library, and finish your class work; you must strive for excellence and always do your best to get good grades. Don't be afraid to ask questions to your teachers in order to better understand your lessons. After high school, you can go to university and choose for example the faculties of: Science, Medicine, Law, Humanities, etc.

Bill, Angela, Haneul: Thank you Aya for your advice! You just told us some very interesting and important things! Nothing to add. It is well said!

Bill: It is already time to go home. Our parents are waiting for us. We will continue our conversation tomorrow.

The next day, during recess time, the three friends meet in the schoolyard.

Bill: Guys, do you know that when I came home last night, I told my aunt Fatima what Aya told us yesterday. After that, my aunt told me a story about an immigrant woman who had a part time job at the Pearson Airport and was studying at the same time. She worked very hard to finish her studies and today she is now a professor of physics at Harvard University in the United States.

Angela: What a brave and brilliant woman!

Bill: It is true! If she can do it, we can achieve our dreams too.

Haneul: Surely! I think we need a lot of possible advices to accomplish our dreams.

Bill: You are right. You know that my aunt Fatima often encourages me to study well in class so that later I can become an astronomer or astronaut and have everything I need. She lives with us and she often reminds me of the Quebec proverb that says: "Time passes and does not return". That is why every time I get home from school, she often encourages me to review what I studied in class, do my homework or finish my projects.

My aunt gives me advice to behave well in class, to be always on time and willing to learn, to be polite to my teachers, and to be nice to my classmates. She tells me to participate often in class, to share my ideas, to ask questions every time when there are things I don't understand, to organize my things well, not to disturb in class, to cooperate well with other students.

My aunt often encourages me to work hard to get good grades in class. She advises me not to be absent when I am not sick, to listen carefully when the teacher is explaining lessons, projects and activities.

She often tells me that I am capable of being whatever I dream to become in future, and that takes courage, and hard work.

Angela: Can I also tell you what I think?

Haneul: Well Angela, go ahead, we are listening.

Angela: After talking to Aya, I find that to achieve a goal, one must persevere even if it takes a little time! I am very young to have all the information about our dream jobs, but at least I often know that university degrees require a lot of time and effort. To be a great scientist, an astronomer/astronaut, a neurologist, a pediatrician, a cardiologist, a lawyer, a pilot, an architect, a writer, etc., you have to **have big dreams**! You have to put in a lot of effort! Nothing is impossible! We should strive for excellence in everything we do.

Bill: After all the conversations we had, I think we know what to expect to achieve our dreams. So, friends, let's do our best!

Title : Having Big Dreams! What does It take to become...? Written by Eugénie Mujawiyera ; illustrated by Chris Rutayisire

Text copyright©2022 by Eugénie Mujawiyera (Eugeniebooks15@gmail.com)
Illustrations copyright©2022 by Chris Rutayisire ((rutayichris@gmail.com)

All rights reserved

This book can be used by elementary students: from grade 4 to grade 8. Age: from 9 to 14 years old.

It can also be used by teachers (elementary school) or parents to motivate students/children to study hard.

www.ingramcontent.com/pod-product-compliance
Lightning Source LLC
Chambersburg PA
CBHW051324110526
44590CB00031B/4458